THERAPY
FOR
HUMANS

BASED ON DOG'S ADVICE

BILL GRIFFIN

PR MIX
PUBLISHING
THE WRITE CHOICE

Primix Publishing
11620 Wilshire Blvd
Suite 900, West Wilshire Center, Los Angeles, CA, 90025
www.primixpublishing.com
Phone: 1-800-538-5788

Published by Primix Publishing   09/16/2021

ISBN: 978-1-955944-14-4(sc)
ISBN: 978-1-955944-15-1(e)

Library of Congress Control Number: 2021920091

This book is dedicated to

TONY
An Akita/Shepherd Mix
who loved everyone

Because it was difficult to type with those big
paws, he dictated the knowledge in this book

To
Bill Griffin
His Human

TABLE OF CONTENTS

CANINE EVALUATION OF HUMAN STRESS 1

AREAS OF STRESS 3

CERTIFICATE 20

EPILOGUE 21

CANINE EVALUATION
OF HUMAN STRESS

After years of observation, we canines have
concluded that Humans need a lot of therapy.

Do cellphones really have all the answers to life?

So we put our minds together and decided
to pick areas causing stress.
The only way to communicate this much-needed stress-relief
therapy was by comparing canine and human behavior.

Study these carefully and you will relieve your stress
and anxieties, so you can live a full and happy life.

AREAS OF STRESS

RELAXATION

COMMUNICATION

FRIENDS

EXCITEMENT ABOUT THE DAY

FINDING TIME TO PLAY

NAPS

BELIEVING IN YOUR DREAMS

PURSUING KNOWLEDGE

BORING COMPANY

REJECTION

SECURITY

NO . . .

A DAY AT THE BEACH

DOWN DAYS HAPPEN

FOOD DISCUSSIONS

RELAXATION

HUMANS DO THIS

Four-step deep breathing

Yoga

Muscle by muscle relaxation

Visualization

Stretching

CANINES DO THIS

Climb onto the couch

Circle three times

Just breathe in the relaxation

Trying to do all those human things "correctly" just adds to their stress

COMMUNICATION

HUMANS DO THIS	CANINES DO THIS
Tend to ignore obvious signs	Are quite clear on what we want
Talk on their cell phone	Maybe I should learn how to text
Watch TV and not aware it is past my dinner time	Bang the empty dinner bowel around
Need a cup of coffee first	Coffee will taste better after we get back
Get annoyed if we take too long to check a smell	Need to check our "pee-mail"
Say we have already had a treat today	Lay in the middle of the kitchen floor immediately following dinner

FRIENDS

HUMANS DO THIS

Seem to have strong need
to impress friends

Like company when they eat

Sometimes talk loudly
and continuously

Hope friends will accept
their way of doing things

Sometimes argue with friends

CANINES DO THIS

Every canine is a possible
friend. Greet and sniff

Not real keen on sharing food

Barking may be necessary to
communicate an important issue

Don't care if ball or stick
has slobber on it

Don't carry a grudge if
someone barks at us

EXCITEMENT ABOUT THE DAY

HUMANS DO THIS

Getting up in the morning seems to require grumbling

Deciding what to wear takes time

Look at the clock frequently

Anxiety seems to replace Excitement

CANINES DO THIS

Breakfast will be coming

Wear the same thing every day and nobody seems concerned

Maybe If I watch the clock, we could go on a walk sooner

New smells, new adventures, nap

FINDING TIME TO PLAY

HUMANS DO THIS	CANINES DO THIS
Must schedule it for a specific time and place	Every day, anywhere, anytime is a good time to play
Have discussions about the rules of play	Just throw the frisbee
Laugh, yell, argue and knock each other to the ground	Bark to let them know you are still waiting for someone to throw the frisbee
Get annoyed if dogs try to join in their game	I got it and now you have to chase me. That is my rule

NAPS

HUMANS DO THIS

Work must be exhausting or boring, because they nap right at their desk. Looks very uncomfortable

Refer to something called "A power nap"

Probably should stop watching The Late Late Show

Go to sleep on the couch

CANINES DO THIS

Naps are best if you have a special place

Take a "catnap" (hate that term) referring to light sleep

Much more beneficial to sleep than to watch TV

Go to sleep on the couch

BELIEVING IN YOUR DREAMS

HUMANS DO THIS

Dream big. Sent a man to the moon. Must not have liked him much

Dream about getting bigger things

Sometimes forget that love and companionship make dreams come true

Seems like children believe in their dreams better than adults

CANINES DO THIS

Not interested in being the first dog in space. Let the monkeys have that honor

A small hole is all that is needed to bury a bone

Our dreams are simple: walk, treat, petting, nap. What else would you dream about?

He told me to go get a stick. He does not realize I am Superdog

PURSUING KNOWLEDGE

HUMANS DO THIS

Get their knowledge from
TV, computers and cell
phones. causing reactions
from happiness
to annoyance

Get knowledge from talking to
each other. This is surprising
because most are talking
and few are listening

Their opinions are right.
No need to consider
another's knowledge

Some insist their dog is
smarter than your dog

CANINES DO THIS

Are naturally curious. Do we miss
any smells on our walks ---No

If there is anything new
in the house or yard, we
immediately check it out

Mostly listen for words like walk,
dinner, treat. Sometimes have
to bark to explain our wants

Research has refuted the
claim that Felines are
superior to Canines

BORING COMPANY

HUMANS DO THIS	CANINES DO THIS
Try to be polite and hide their yawn	Big yawn
Head dropping and eyelids closing	Ask if they want to play
Suddenly realize the person has stopped talking	Talk about treats or walks
Are embarrassed	Either walk away or take a nap
Person that was talking is annoyed	

REJECTION

HUMANS DO THIS	CANINES DO THIS
Get mad	Wag our tail in friendship
Blame everyone else	Give a second chance to pet us
Feel mis-understood	If not wanted, we go away
Complain about the attitude of some people	Probably pee on the new tire on your car as we leave

SECURITY

HUMANS DO THIS

Buy $1000 of locks and alarms

Monitor their home frequently on their cell phones

Accidently alert the police while trying to unlock the door

Never give me credit for standing guard all day

CANINES DO THIS

Show teeth, growl and bark loudly

Jump at the window and watch the the intruder run away fast

Let me out so I can go after that bad guy

If he had a steak, I would welcome him in

NO . . .

HUMANS DO THIS	CANINES DO THIS
Yell at me and look for my owner to yell at him too	Wondering why that woman is yelling at me
Calling the Dog Impound	I can't read. Doesn't the sign mean sit here?
Getting red in the face	She probably has a cat and does not like dogs
Pointing me out to other people	Maybe I should move closer to the sign

A DAY AT THE BEACH

HUMANS DO THIS

Bring the whole house, clothes, toys, shade umbrella, sun screen, food, drinks, chairs, ...

Sit in their chairs

Wander down to the water's edge

Sit and drink

Check their cell phone

Humans holding their noses and pointing at me

CANINES DO THIS

Just bring my water and food dish

Clear the beach of all those annoying birds

Drink the salt water and throw up

Dig right next to their sandcastle

What is that heavenly smell - a rotting seal carcass. Roll and rub it into my fur

I can show them where the carcass is so they can enjoy it too

DOWN DAYS HAPPEN

HUMANS DO THIS	CANINES DO THIS
Go to the bathroom, call in sick and go back to bed	Really need to be a lap dog, regardless of size
Get a cup of coffee and realize there is no milk for the coffee or cereal	Need to be petted more than usual A treat or walk would make me feel better
Turn on the TV Turn off the TV	What's wrong with having a soggy half-chewed bone on the couch
Cough and share their germs	No, I don't want to go to the Vet

FOOD DISCUSSIONS

HUMANS DO THIS

Fret about the calories
in each food

Every morning they
step on a scale and say
some muffled words

Say people food is not good
for dogs, yet they eat it

CANINES DO THIS

What are calories? Do
they taste like chicken?

Then they cut back on my snacks

We are expected to eat
tasteless food with peas in it

CERTIFICATE OF COMPLETION

This Certificate is presented to:

For successful completion of the

Therapy for Humans

Paw Print

Date

EPILOGUE

SHARE YOUR DAY

CPSIA information can be obtained
at www.ICGtesting.com
Printed in the USA
BVHW021529050422
633360BV00005B/119

9 781955 944144